ANDREA PISTOLESI

VANCOUVER
SUNRISE TO SUNSET

Text by
GIORGIO BIZZI
and
MARIE LUTTRELL

BONECHI

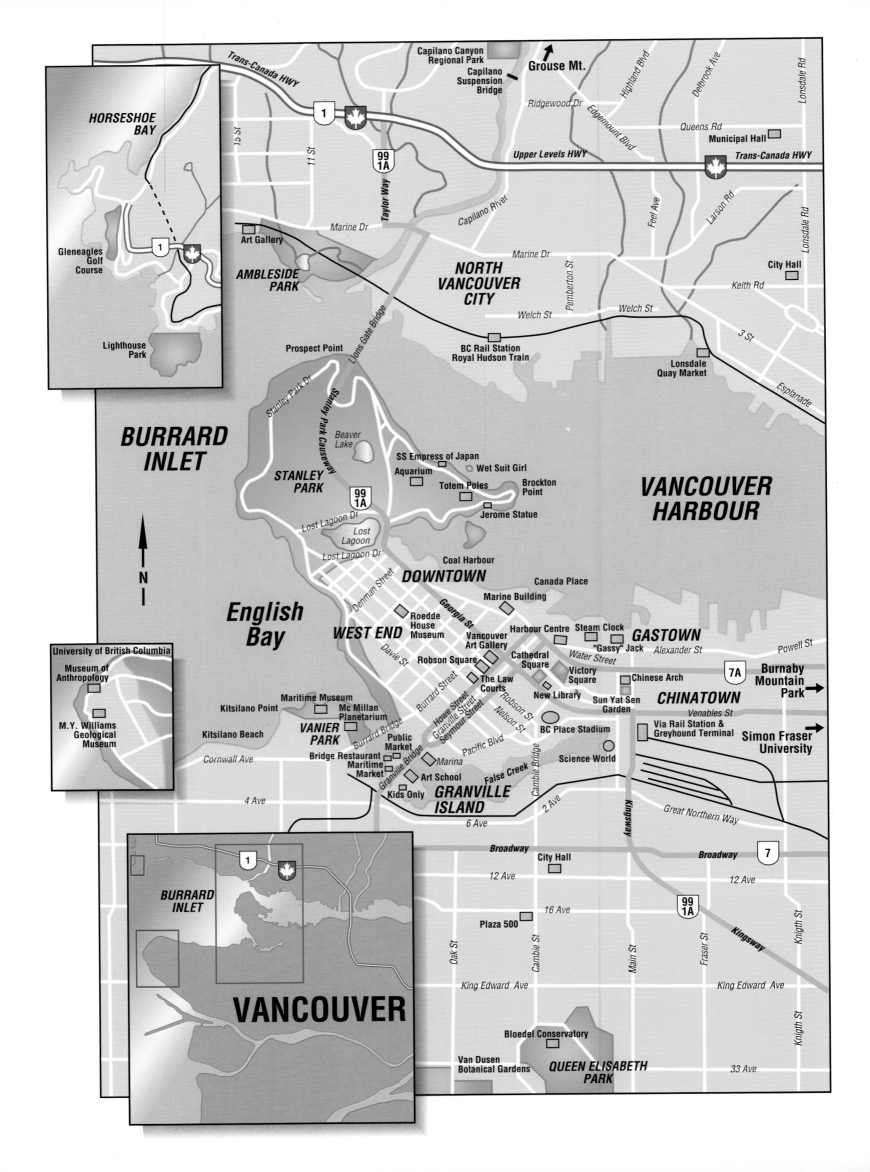

Contents

Introduction

Few cities are so immediately attractive that the casual visitor is actually tempted to move there permanently. Vancouver, according to its inhabitants, is one of those rare cities. It is quite normal to hear people who have been living there for only a few months already describing themselves as Vancouverites. Tourists have been known to go straight from the hotel to a real estate agency to check on the possibility of moving there. The southern coast of British Columbia, where Vancouver is located, enjoys a mild climate due to warm ocean currents from Japan. Although Vancouver has the reputation of being a wet city, rain falls mainly in winter. With the mountains overlooking the city, one can be on the ski slopes within minutes of the city centre. In fact, in Spring you can ski in the morning, sail at lunch and play golf in the afternoon. Outdoor recreation is highly valued with hundreds of tennis courts, many fine private and public golf courses, and miles and miles of trails through woodland or near water for walking and cycling. With Vancouver Island sheltering the South Coast from the battering of the Pacific, the opportunities for all sorts of fishing and boating abound. That same shelter has made the Port of Vancouver the busiest port on the west coast of North America, shipping grains, lumber and raw materials all over the Asia Pacific region. High tech business has seen a recent boom, and Vancouver has earned the title "Hollywood North" because of a flourishing movie and television industry.

Add to all this a well-established and advanced social welfare system and tight control over urban planning and private and public architectural initiatives, and it is perhaps no surprise that present day Vancouver has been compared to San Francisco in the 1960's and '70's - a sort of Mecca for those who seek both a high standard in working conditions and a high-quality life style.

Previous and following pages - Vancouver features a Native American legacy, modern architecture, outdoor life.

B.C. Place Stadium and General Motors Place, which house Vancouver's professional sports teams stand at the gateway to downtown Vancouver's business core.

COAL HARBOUR

Downtown Vancouver lies on a peninsula at about the mid-point of the city itself. The North shore of this peninsula is formed by Coal Harbour, its shoreline graced with walking trails, marinas, and downtown hotels. A seaside

walkway will soon surround the entire downtown core. Adjoining the business and residential areas is historic Stanley Park, a 1000 acre playground of gardens, old growth forest, and recreational facilities.

A romantic view of Downtown at night, from Coal Harbour. In the middle, the unmistakable tower of the Harbour Centre Observation Deck offers a dramatic sight of the entire city from its revolving restaurant.

CANADA PLACE

F rom mid-May to mid-September, Canada Place is the launching point for Alaska Cruises, with ships arriving early each morning and departing in the evening. Its unique roof structure has become a symbol of Vancouver.

A vast galleon with its sails spread wide. That was the theme that inspired the plan of Canada Place, opened in 1986 to host the Canadian pavillion of the Expo, as a reminder of the city's maritime history. The overall effect is that of a gigantic ship in full sail. The maritime theme is further emphasized by the presence of luxurious cruise ships which berth here.

15

*F*ull sunlight, the glow of sunset, or
multicoloured lights at night play with
striking effects over the "sails" of Canada Place.

*C*anada Place stretches out into the harbour
like a romantic ocean liner.

THE MARINE BUILDING

*T*he Marine Building, at 355 Burrard Street was built in 1929 and demonstrates the amazingly detailed craftsmanship of its Art Déco design. With its polished brass motifs and mosaic inlaid floors, visitors even just to the lobby of the building stand in awe of its ornate beauty.

"...it is like a rock, rising from the sea, covered with marine flora and fauna...and dusted with gold". Thus its designers, McCarter and Nairne described the Marine Building, an elegant and varied structure climbing up to a single pinnacle, sited at 355 Burrard Street. Built in Art Déco style in 1929, it is one of the most famous buildings in the city. At the time of its construction, it was also the tallest building in Vancouver.

RUN, MAN, RUN!

Sporting Clubs have been part of the history of Vancouver for a century, with sports like track and field, rugby, curling, basketball, or hockey, among many others. This statue in Stanley Park

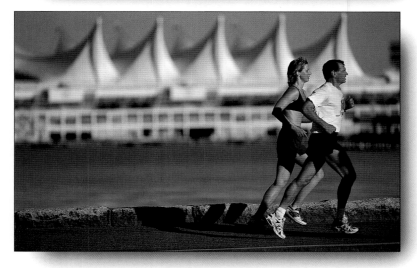

commemorates one of Vancouver's greatest athletes, Harry Jerome. Named British Columbia's Athlete of the Century in its centennial year of 1971, he was once the "fastest man in the world".

THE NATIVE AMERICAN LEGACY

For thousands of years, the Coast Salish people lived in the area of Vancouver, with village sites marked by the longhouses and totems. Totems represented the families and tribes much like a crest, the symbols of animals interrelating their lives to the natural world. The crow, the beaver, the wolf, fox, whale, eagle, and so on each carried with them a spirituality intrinsic to the native way of life.

*T*ies to the Orient have been essential to
 the history of Vancouver since its
inception. With the completion of the
Railway in the 1880's the natural trading
routes to the Asia Pacific countries became
an important feature of Vancouver's
economy. The Empress line of merchant
clipper ships, named for Queen Victoria as
Empress of India, plied these trade routes
from the 1890's to the 1920's. The
figurehead of one of those early ships adorns
the scenic drive through Stanley Park,
reminding visitors and Vancouverites of the
multi-cultural origins of the present city.

THE AQUARIUM

The killer whale, the best known large mammal of the Pacific Ocean, is the star of the Aquarium, along with the enormous, gentle beluga, a type of whale quite common in Arctic waters also known as the 'sea canary', due to the wide range of sounds it is capable of reproducing. The Vancouver Aquarium also hosts various ecosystems recreated in several sections within it. One, for example, is dedicated to the Amazonian Rain Forest, which houses piranha, anaconda and birds, and another to the environment of the Tropical Pacific with the coral reefs of the Hawaiin Islands and Australia. However, the largest section is obviously that representing the coasts of British Columbia and the Canadian Arctic.

APPROACHING
THE TOWN
FROM THE SEA

"... watching the ships roll in... watching the tide". The magnificent glow of the sunset over the Pacific Ocean is not seen here from the Dock of the Bay, but from Burrard Inlet, crossed by the Lions Gate Bridge. This suspension bridge, carrying traffic on its three lanes, connects North and West Vancouver. The bridge, named for the majestic twin "Lion's Peaks" in the North shore mountains, is the city's gateway and, at 60 metres in height, allows the greatest ships to pass beneath it.

*T*he Capilano Canyon, created by the Capilano river, marks the borderline between North and West Vancouver. It is an exciting experience to cross the canyon by the Capilano Suspension Bridge, a narrow, swinging footbridge, 137 metres long and 70 metres above the luxuriant vegetation of the canyon and the river below. The first bridge, consisting simply of taut rope cables, was made in 1889.

The present structure was built in the 1950's and consists of steel cable, anchored at both ends by 13 tons of cement.

33

PRESERVING TRADITION

In the 1930's, Chief Mathias Joe Capilano began to carve the totems seen near the Capilano Suspension Bridge in order to preserve a unique and precious heritage. Native carvers today still learn and practice the ancient skill.

COLOURFUL NEIGHBOURHOODS

I It doesn't take long to discover in Vancouver some of her hidden treasures - her variety of neighbourhoods which range from cultural to playful to avant-garde. On Denman Street, the whimsy of a

movie-star mural is only blocks away from the haute-mode shopping district. Victoria Drive is home to the earthy counter culture, with coffee houses and lovely side streets. One short street here posts a sign: "Welcome to Rose Street." Pockets of Vietnamese, Indian, or Korean populations have brought stores and restaurants which open Vancouver to new foods and products and a vast range of cultural festivals and ways of life.

A RAINY TOWN?

In the summertime, just a few yards from home, one can relax in the sun on the most pleasant west coast 'Riviera' beach where the sea is dotted with the brightly coloured sails of windsurfers.

*T*he presence of groups of musicians, buskers,
mimers, acrobats and street artists on almost
every corner and in many of the cafés too, some of
which organize their own programme of concerts,
provides relaxing entertainment for bypassers and
audiences alike.

A GREAT PLACE
TO LIVE

The West End, an area wedged between the downtown business section and Stanley Park, is true city living. Tree-lined streets with apartment buildings, both low and high rise, fill this most densely populated of all areas in the city. People who live here love the convenience of walking to work, to shop, to the theatre, or to the water. 1000 acre Stanley Park is at their doorsteps, and even a stroll through the neighbourhoods brings a delightful blend of new and old.

English Bay stretches from the south side of this region to Georgia Strait and is home in the summer to the "Symphony of Fire", an international competition of fireworks displays set to music. Hundreds of thousands come each summer to see this spectacular display.

43

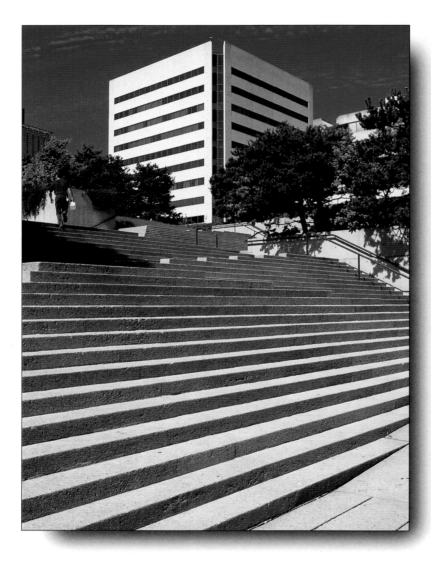

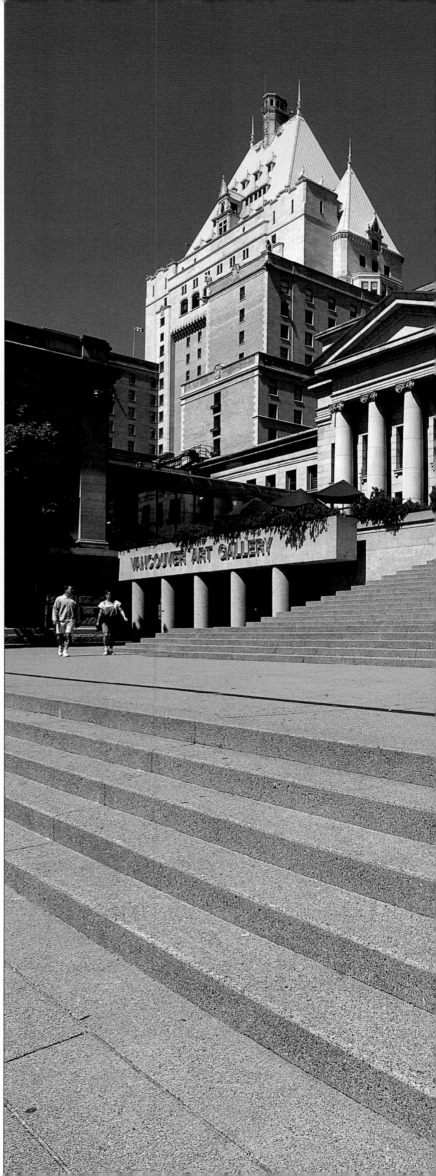

*T*he lowest level of Robson Square,
partially covered by domes made
of dark glass and metal, contrasts
with the Neoclassic style of the Art Gallery,
but blends with the modern design
of the Law Courts.

ROBSON SQUARE

Robson Square is an entirely pedestrian zone and is Vancouver's most popular meeting place. Built on several levels, the lowest, beneath street level, houses shops, restaurants and cafés. The Vancouver Art Gallery, dated 1909, was originally the old courthouse of British Columbia. It houses works by Canadian and international artists and the largest collection of works by Emily Carr, the best known British Columbian artist. Particularly famous are the Law Courts, opened in 1979, whose modern structure slopes down towards Robson Square in an imaginative series of steps and chutes with flowing water.

45

ROBSON STREET

In the late 1960's, one could visit Robson Street and find any number of German restaurants. Today, it is a place to see and be seen, with coffee shops, restaurants and shops to rival Rodeo Drive in Beverly Hills.

A favorite spot for tourists, it is the best place in town for people watching. At night, it takes on a festive atmosphere, and is always bustling with people heading for their favorite night club or restaurant.

*T*he Vancouver Public Library main branch occupies a city block between Georgia and Robson Streets in the heart of the entertainment area. Its large entryway and enclosed concourse naturally invite people to come and browse.

THE
NEW LIBRARY

Vancouver's new Public Library, opened in 1995, lies on the west side of the area known as the Robson Strip, one of the newer districts of the city. Inspired by the Colosseum in Rome as it stands today, the building is as elegant and varied as it is intriguing. Built of pink stone, the rooms inside are perfectly lit by the enormous glass windows which, due to the circular design of the building, provide direct light at all hours of the day. 49

THE MYTHICAL GUARDIAN

According to Indian legend, the entrance to the bay is guarded by a crab, and the Pacific Space Centre, suitably shaped like a flying saucer, is guarded by an enormous metal crab, a sculpture by George Norris.

CITY HALL

Vancouver's City Hall was built in the 1930's, in the middle of the Depression and became a symbol of the vitality of a city. At the time, a sixth of the population was living beneath subsistence level, nevertheless, the city persevered with the building of its Hall. In 1936, fifty years after the founding of the city, the building was completed, admirably simple and pure in design, architecturally a mix of modern Neoclassic and Art Déco.

KITSILANO BEACH

Of the many beaches in the city of Vancouver, Kitsilano Beach, is probably the best known. Adjoined by a large green park, its features have lured people for 60 years - warm water, sandy beach, great fish and chips, a freshwater pool, and Kitsilano Showboat. The Showboat has been in use every summer since 1935, providing visitors to its amphitheatre free entertainment.

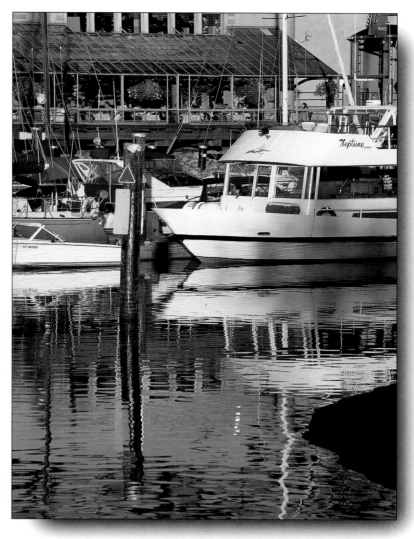

AN ISLAND
OF LEISURE
AND PLEASURE

Where once industrial warehouses stood along the wharfs, today there are cafés and restaurants, directly overlooking the ships and boats, giving visitors a real feeling of seafaring life. This is Granville Island, perhaps Vancouver's most fashionable restaurant district, where locals like to bring visiting friends to try the renowned seafood cooking. The combination of the well equipped Marina and the restaurants, theatres, crafts shops and artists' studios give Granville Island the unique and fascinating atmosphere of both a practical working port with, however, a sophisticated flavour.

Not to be missed is the Public Market, more like a treasure trove for gourmets and a well stocked bazaar, than any normal agricultural foodmarket. Locals, as well as those who come to shop from more distant parts of town, are able to find all kinds of specialities here, from fresh vegetables to seafood, from the exotic spices needed for ethnic cuisine, to rare imported wines, from fresh pasta to over 150 different types of cheese.

FALSE CREEK

False Creek is a very short inlet mistaken for a creek by the Royal Navy when originally charting the area and named 'false' as a result of the error. When, however, Vancouver began to extend to the south, the continual need to skirt around the far end of False Creek became increasingly inconvenient and finally in 1932 Burrard Street Bridge was built near the mouth of the inlet.

Thus Burrard Street with its bridge crosses the entire city centre as far as the port, where Canada Place now is, and provides a speedy link to the south side of the city. The bridge has a central steel span, typical of the engineering of the period, and entering it one passes beneath elegant arches built in Art Déco style at both ends.

OUTDOOR LIVING IS MORE FUN

Vancouver happily combines the natural tendency towards physical exercise inherited from a pioneering past with the recent mania for health and fitness. City founders wisely set aside ample space for parks, green spaces and water access. At any one time, one might find people jogging or cycling, lawn bowling, golfing, playing slow-pitch softball or beach volleyball, kayaking, or practicing karate. The local mountains are used year round for skiing, snow-boarding and hiking or mountain biking.

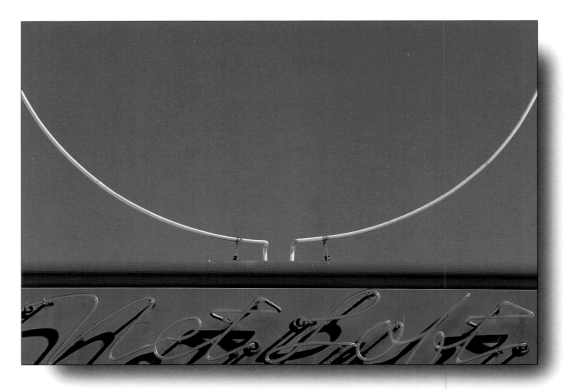

THE MONTMARTRE OF VANCOUVER

Nestled in a corner of Granville Island where foundries once made chains and cement plants shipped limestone, the Emily Carr Institute of Art and Design has risen to become one of Canada's leading schools of art. It was named for Emily Carr, a pioneering painter whose broad lines and bold colours depicted the rugged beauty of British Columbia.

Granville Island marinas are well equipped with everything necessary for yachts, sailboats or smaller pleasure craft. Boaters will often pull into a berth just long enough to tuck into a specialty at one of the many area restaurants. Even a tiny aquabus makes regular passenger runs across False Creek.

SCIENCE WORLD

The splendid geodesic dome of Science World rests on 182 pillars and is 155 feet high. The exterior of the building consists of 766 panels of stainless steel sheathing and has 391 lights. The interior is an immense 10,220 square metres altogether, with the Alcan Omnimax Theatre at the top. This incredible theatre, which seats 400 people, features all-round sound and a screen which is equal to five storeys in height.

CHINATOWN

Chinatown means pavements crowded until late at night, brightly coloured neon lights, constant traffic jams. It is a city within a city and an important part of Vancouver's history, as well as one of the oldest districts in the city. In the local shops you can buy all manner of specialities from foodstuffs to antique porcelain. At the entrance to the area in Pender Street is the Chinese Cultural Centre, the most important symbol of Chinatown's identity, in front of which stands the monumental entrance to the Chinese Pavillon made for Expo '86 and afterwards given to the Chinese community as proof of the continuing strong links with the homeland. The entire area is now considered a national monument.

If one happens to visit Chinatown around January or February (the date varies depending on the lunar calendar) he may see the colourful Chinese New Year celebrations which last from three days to a week.

73

A MING GARDEN

This magnificent garden in Ming style is dedicated to the first president of China, Sun-Yat-Sen, who came here in 1911 to collect funds for the Kuomintang from the large Chinese community of Vancouver.

GASTOWN

Gastown, which owes its name to 'Gassy' Jack Deighton, the founder of the very first saloon in Vancouver, forms the historic centre of the city of Vancouver. On a stretch of several blocks near the downtown waterfront, the streets and sidewalks are paved with brick. Some of Vancouver's original warehouse and commercial buildings were refurbished and now draw local and tourist alike to visit unique shops, restaurants and galleries. Merchants sell foods and products from all over the world, while the many Galleries sell some of the finest collections of sculptures and prints by indigenous artists.

An intriguing clock, driven by a steam mechanism, stands in the heart of Gastown. Made in 1977 by clockmaker Ray Saunders, the steam clock is driven by a mechanism designed in 1875. Every hour the steam from an underground system, sets off a series of whistles while a music box inside the clock plays the chimes of Big Ben every quarter of an hour.

G assy Jack's Saloon opened in 1867 and became so infamous that in the 1970's a monument to 'Gassy Jack', the hero who gave his name to the early pioneering town, standing on a barrel of the whisky he sold, was unveiled on the original site.

77

"THE PLAYGROUND OF THE GODS"
In 1989, Burnaby's sister city of Kushiro, Japan presented this group of totem poles to commemorate 25 years of good will. The poles were carved by Matzuri Toko to represent the animals and birds which are powerful symbols to the Ainu, the aboriginal people of Hokkaido.

A TROPICAL DOME

In 1969, the Bloedel Conservatory was built in Queen Elizabeth Park, its futuristic design anticipating many of those structures later built for Expo '86. Inside the hothouse, brightly coloured birds fly freely and in the specially recreated habitat over five hundred species of tropical flowers and plants are kept.

84

The Museum of Anthropology, inspired by the traditional style of Northwest coastal Indian building, emphasizes the grandeur and complex nature of the indigenous cultures, almost completely eliminated by the European immigrants. Displayed are the various structures found in Indian villages, original totem poles dating from the end of the 19th century, crockery, ritual masks and jewellery.

DOCK HERE AND FIND EVERYTHING

Right on the port of North Vancouver – cluttered wharfs, cranes and merchant ships at dock –, the Lonsdale Quay Market sells goods of all kinds, from agricultural produce such as fresh fruit and vegetables, to fish, lobster, oysters and meat, but also imported food specialities, and even jewellery and fashion clothing elegantly displayed in little shops in balconies above. Cafés and restaurants are plentiful and there is a hotel on the upper level.

*T*he lighthouse at Point Atkinson, the furthest point of West Vancouver, from which one overlooks the Strait of Georgia and Vancouver Island.

GROUSE MOUNTAIN

The Superskyride – the largest cable car of North America, capable of carrying one hundred people –, rises in a breathtakingly steep climb from almost sea level to a height of 1,130 metres on Grouse Mountain.

HORSESHOE BAY

Rounding the bend northward into Howe Sound from West Vancouver, lies Horseshoe Bay, a small community which attracts large numbers of visitors. The spectacular fjord of Howe Sound with snow-capped mountains plunging into the salt waters off Georgia Strait is breathtaking. One can enjoy the beauty from a waterfront park or from a café in the small shopping area. Here, too, is the British Columbia ferry terminal with links to Nanaimo on Vancouver Island, Bowen Island in Howe Sound and the Sunshine Coast on the mainland.

Distributed by
Natural Color Productions
#17, 1610 Derwent Way, Annacis Island
New Westminster, B.C. V3M 6W1
Tel: (604) 521-1579
Fax: (604) 522-0145

Project and editorial conception: Casa Editrice Bonechi
Publication Manager: Monica Bonechi
Picture research: Monica Bonechi
Cover, Graphic design and Make-up: Maria Rosanna Malagrinò
Editing: Simonetta Giorgi
Map: Stefano Benini - Firenze

Text: Giorgio Bizzi, Marie Luttrell
English translation: Eve Leckey

Printed in Italy by Centro Stampa Editoriale Bonechi.

Photographs from archives of Casa Editrice Bonechi taken by
Andrea Pistolesi.

ISBN 88-8029-989-1

*   *   *